1983 limited-edition reproduction of a 1903 teddy bear manufactured by Margarete Steiff and designed by Richard Steiff. Original photograph by Ted Menten.

Handmade "Dorian Gray" teddy bear crafted by Karin Mandell and Howard Calvin of Ballard Baines Bear Co. Original photograph by Ted Menten.

Large rust-colored teddy bear manufactured by Avanti. Original photograph by Ted Menten.

The Margaret Woodbury Strong Museum replica of a 1904 teddy bear manufactured by Margarete Steiff. Original photograph by Ted Menten.

1 *(outside)* Margaret Woodbury Strong Museum replica of a 1904 Steiff bear.
2 *(inside)* Teddy bear manufactured by Avanti.

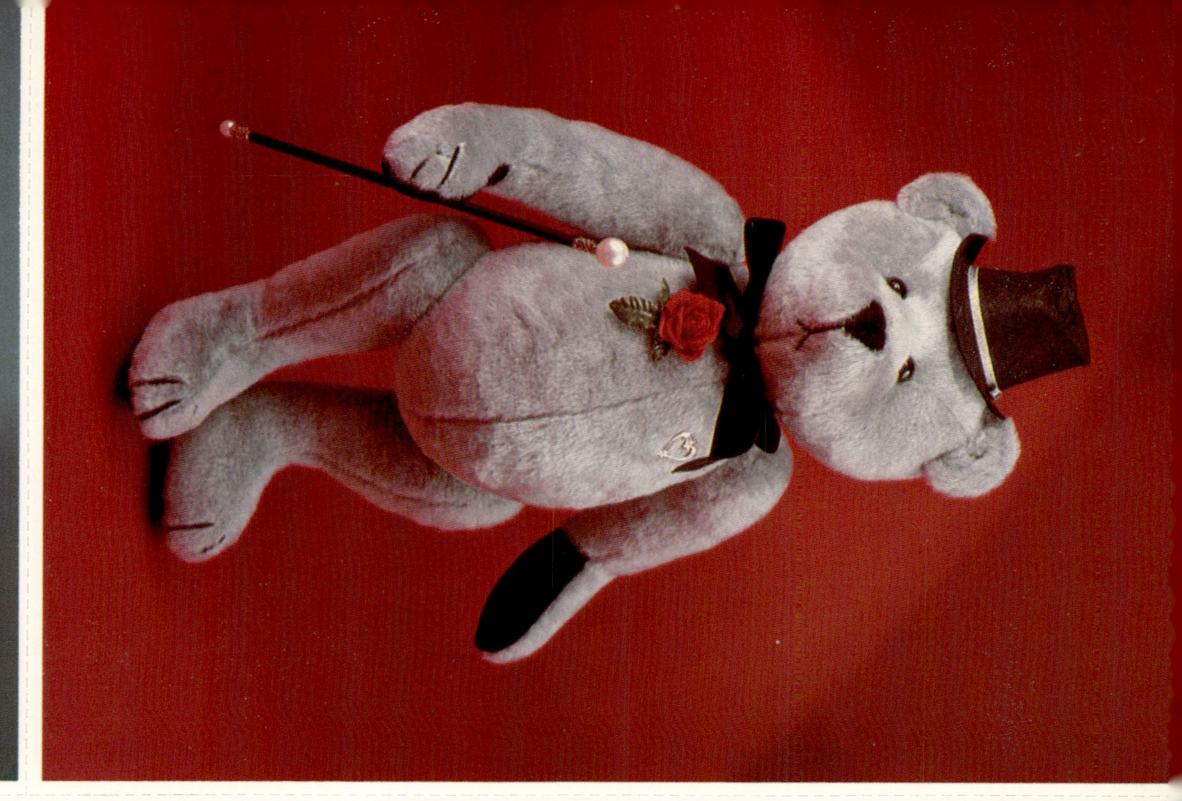

3 *(outside)* Handmade "Dorian Gray" from Ballard Baines Bear Co.
4 *(inside)* Richard Steiff bear, limited-edition reproduction.

5 *(inside)* Bears from Steiff, Hermann and Graham Gridley.
6 *(outside)* Handmade "Graham Gridley."

7 *(inside)* Bears manufactured by Steiff and Hermann.
8 *(outside)* Margaret Woodbury Strong Museum replica of a 1904 Steiff bear.

The Margaret Woodbury Strong Museum replica of a 1904 teddy bear manufactured by Margarete Steiff. Original photograph by Ted Menten.

mall teddy bears manufactured by Steiff and Hermann, wo famous German bear manufacturers. Original photograph by Ted Menten.

From *Teddy Bear Photo Postcards,* © 1985 by Ted Menten

Handmade "Graham Gridley" teddy bear crafted by Mary Olsen of Graham Gridley Bear Co. Original photograph by Ted Menten.

From *Teddy Bear Photo Postcards,* © 1985 by Ted Menten

A group of teddy bears from Steiff, Hermann and Graham Gridley companies wearing handmade sweaters. Original photograph by Ted Menten.

From *Teddy Bear Photo Postcards,* © 1985 by Ted Menten

Handmade teddy bear crafted by Karin Mandell and Howard Calvin of Ballard Baines Bear Co. Original photograph by Ted Menten.

From *Teddy Bear Photo Postcards,* © 1985 by Ted Menten

Handmade "Sir Edward" teddy bear crafted by Terry and Doris Michaud of Carrousel. Original photograph by Ted Menten.

From *Teddy Bear Photo Postcards,* © 1985 by Ted Menten

Large gold "Papa Bear" manufactured by Steiff, white "Teddy" manufactured by Hermann and handmade tiny teddy bear crafted by Anita Holmes. Original photograph by Ted Menten.

From *Teddy Bear Photo Postcards,* © 1985 by Ted Menten

Handmade "Silly Basil" teddy bear crafted by Linda Speigel of Bearly There Company. Original photograph by Ted Menten.

From *Teddy Bear Photo Postcards,* © 1985 by Ted Menten

11 *(outside)* Handmade "Sir Edward" from Carrousel.

12 *(inside)* Handmade bear from Ballard Baines Bear Co.

9 *(outside)* Handmade "Silly Basil" from Bearly There Company.

10 *(inside)* Steiff "Papa Bear," Hermann "Teddy" and tiny bear by Anita Holmes.

15 *(inside)* Richard Steiff bear, limited-edition reproduction.
16 *(outside)* Handmade bear from Ballard Baines Bear Co.

13 *(inside)* Richard Steiff bear, limited-edition reproduction.
14 *(outside)* Handmade bear from Carrousel.

Handmade teddy bear crafted by Karin Mandell and Howard Calvin of Ballard Baines Bear Co. Original photograph by Ted Menten.

1983 limited-edition reproduction of a 1903 teddy bear manufactured by Margarete Steiff and designed by Richard Steiff. Original photograph by Ted Menten.

Handmade teddy bear by Terry and Doris Michaud of Carrousel. Original photograph by Ted Menten.

1983 limited-edition reproduction of a 1903 teddy bear manufactured by Margarete Steiff and designed by Richard Steiff. Original photograph by Ted Menten.

ldy bears manufactured by Steiff, Hermann and Schuco. ginal photograph by Ted Menten.

1983 limited-edition reproductions of a 1903 teddy bear manufactured by Margarete Steiff and designed by Richard Steiff. Original photograph by Ted Menten.

Gold mohair "Teddy" manufactured by Hermann. Original photograph by Ted Menten.

Limited-edition "Maroosuka" teddy bear from "The King's Collection" line, manufactured by Kamar. Original photograph by Ted Menten.

17 *(outside)* "Maroosuka" manufactured by Kamar.

18 *(inside)* Hermann "Teddy."

19 *(outside)* Richard Steiff bears, limited-edition reproductions.

20 *(inside)* Steiff, Hermann and Schuco bears.

23 *(inside)* Margaret Woodbury Strong Museum replicas of a 1904 Steiff bear.
24 *(outside)* "Bunny Basil" and "Silly Basil" from Bearly There Company.

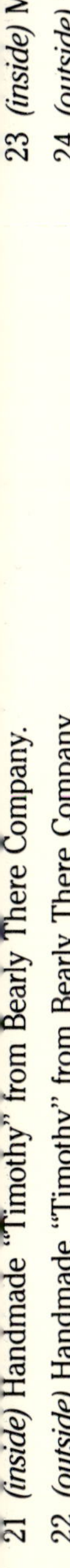
21 *(inside)* Handmade "Timothy" from Bearly There Company.

22 *(outside)* Handmade "Timothy" from Bearly There Company.

Handmade "Bunny Basil" and "Silly Basil" teddy bears crafted by Linda Speigel of Bearly There Company. Original photograph by Ted Menten.

The Margaret Woodbury Strong Museum replicas of a 1904 teddy bear manufactured by Margarete Steiff. Original photograph by Ted Menten.

From *Teddy Bear Photo Postcards,* © 1985 by Ted Menten

Handmade "Timothy" teddy bear crafted by Linda Speigel of Bearly There Company. Original photograph by Ted Menten.

From *Teddy Bear Photo Postcards,* © 1985 by Ted Menten

Handmade "Timothy" teddy bear crafted by Linda Speigel of Bearly There Company. Original photograph by Ted Menten.

From *Teddy Bear Photo Postcards,* © 1985 by Ted Menten